What if?

a book about recycling

Mick Manning and
Brita Granström

W
FRANKLIN WATTS
LONDON • SYDNEY

All sorts of things could happen to a thrown-away bottle. What if, it became a trap for small animals?

What if, it was found a few months later by a famous artist who made it part of a huge sculpture?

What if, the bottle broke? It would take hundreds of sea storms to wear the finger-slicing broken glass into smooth pebbles.

What if, you found the bottle and put a message inside, with a toy boat to stand guard. Then you threw it into the sea?

Long ago, a message in a bottle was the only way people who lived on far-away islands like St. Kilda could contact the mainland.

You should not throw litter into the sea or anywhere else!

What if, the tide carried your bobbing bottle into a whirlpool and it got dragged deep down to the bottom of the sea?

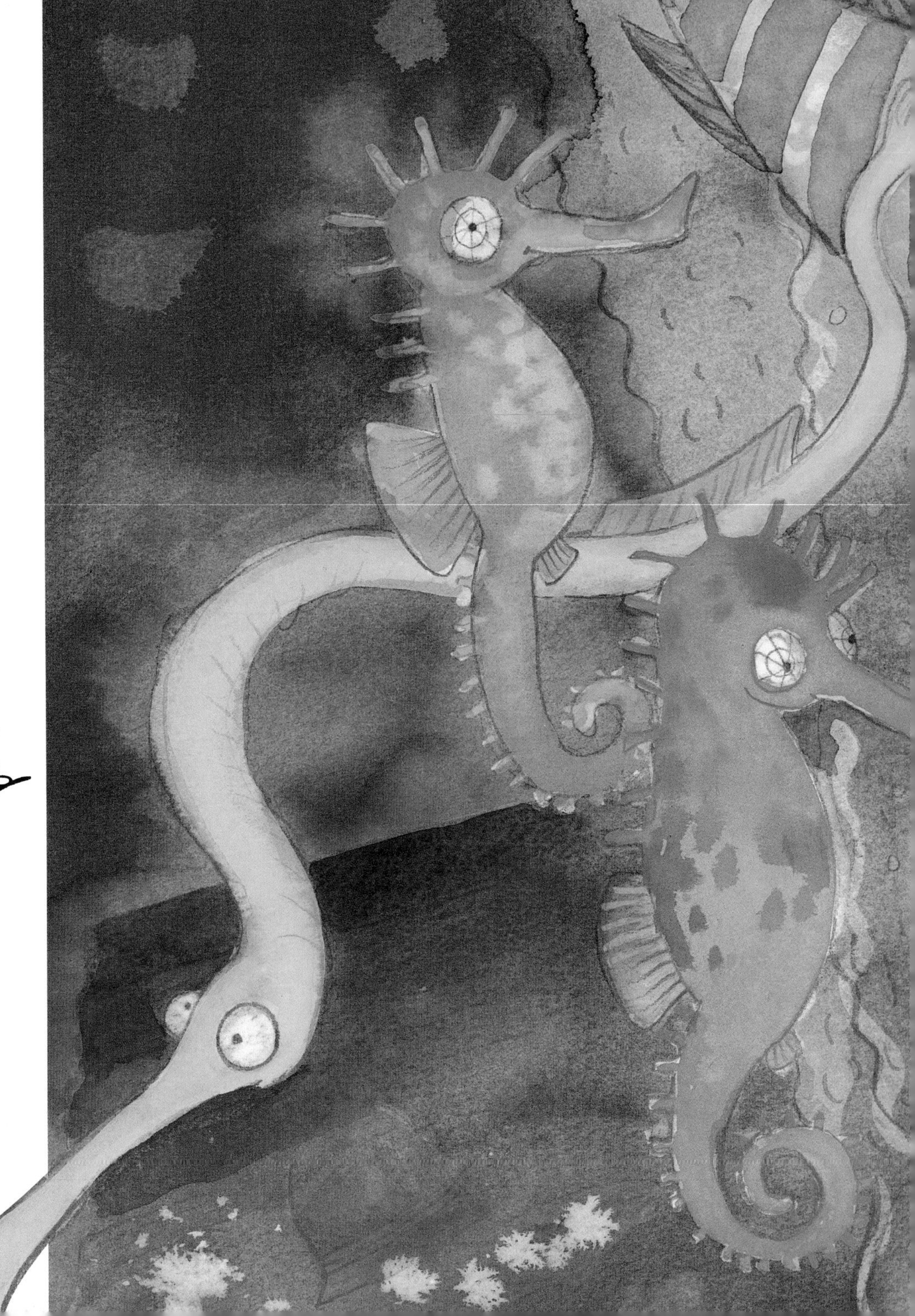

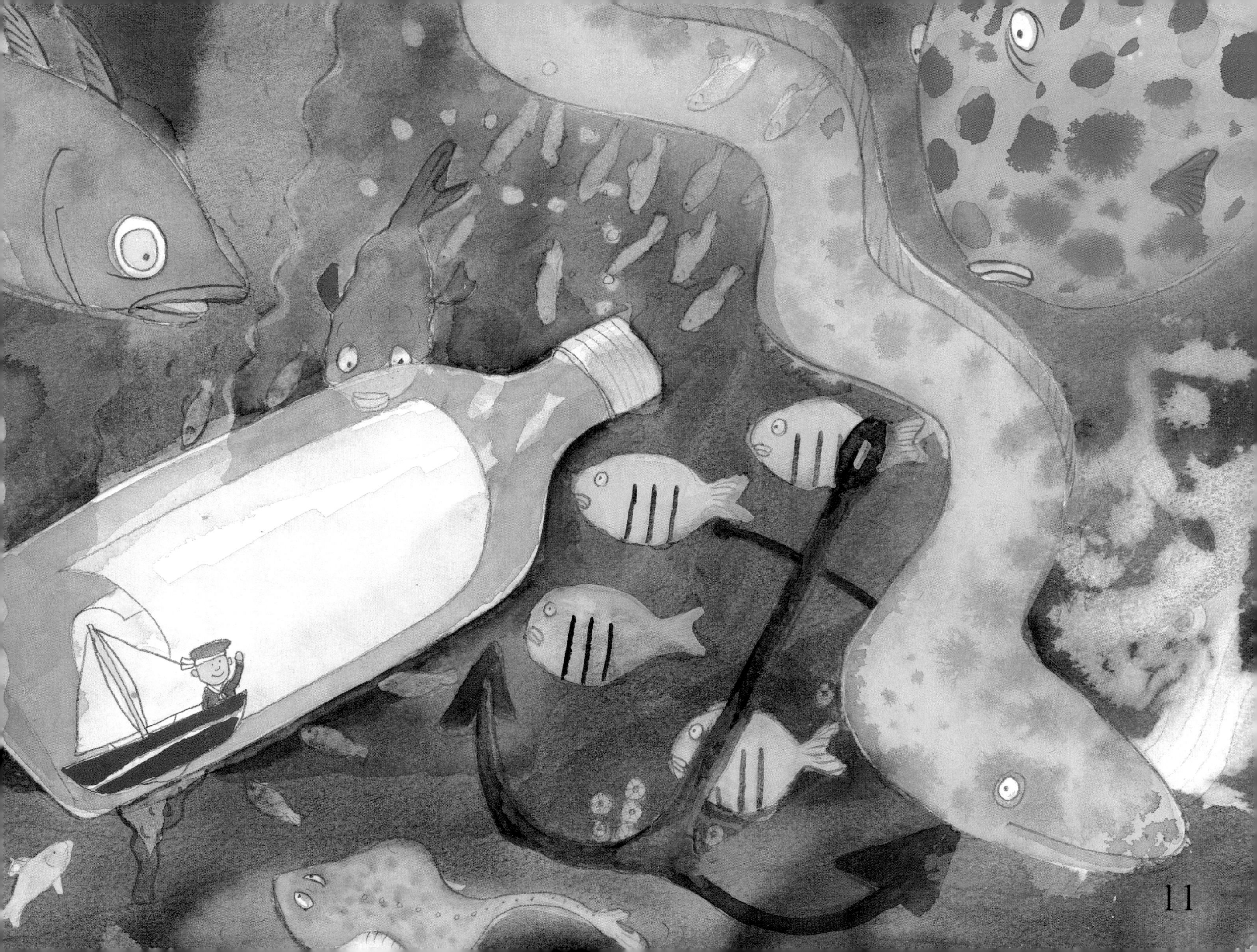

What if, the bottle finally bobbed back up to the surface and sharks poked it curiously with their snouts as it floated on the waves?

Sometimes sharks swallow sharp metal, and turtles will swallow plastic bags thinking they are jellyfish - this can kill them.

plastic bag

jellyfish

turtle

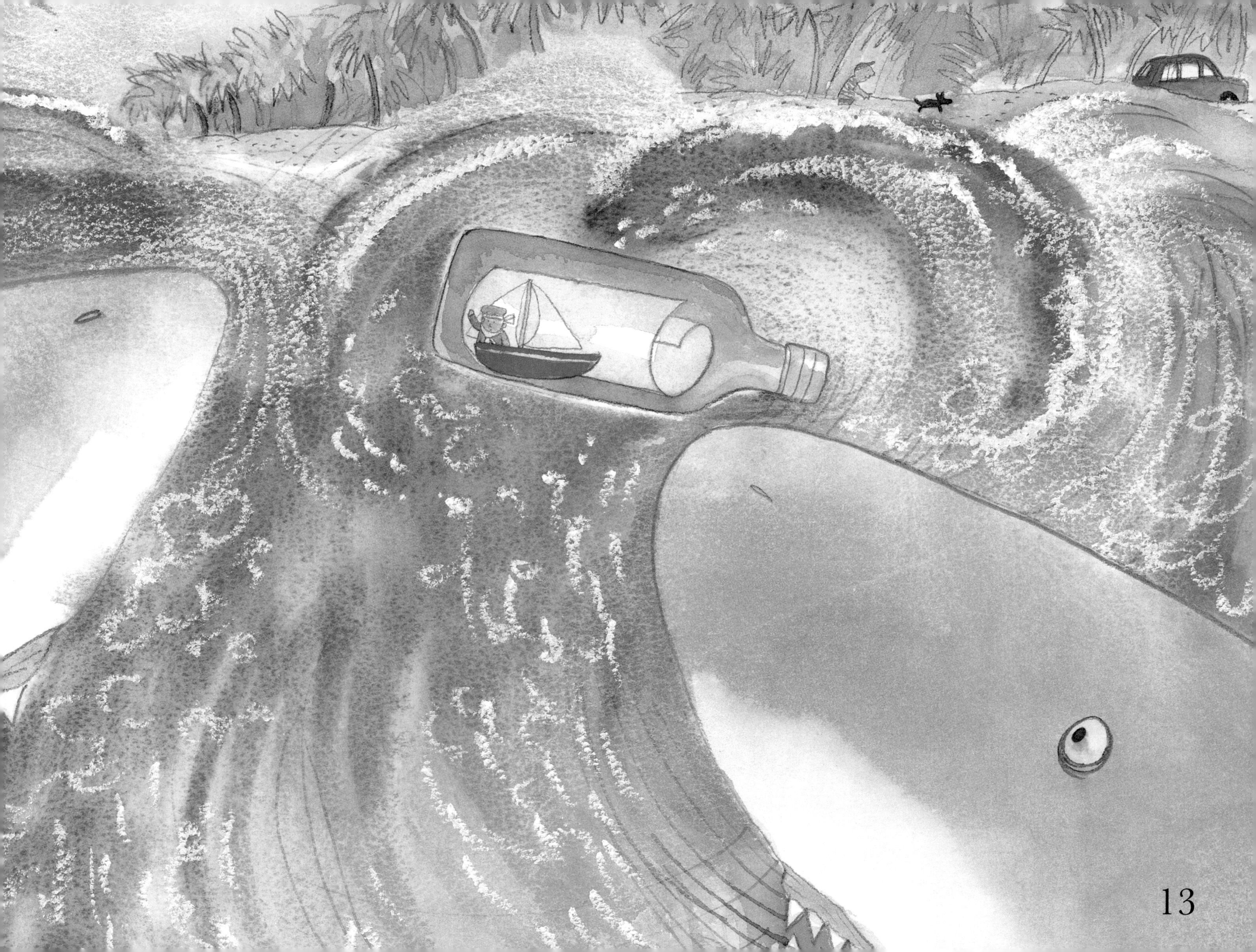

What if, after weeks of drifting across the ocean, your bottle was washed up on a far-away beach?

What if, a beachguard, cleaning up the beach, found the bottle and tossed it into a skip?

Many things can be recycled instead of thrown away, this includes...

What if, the skip was taken by lorry to a recycling plant, where the bottles got sorted and put onto a conveyor belt?

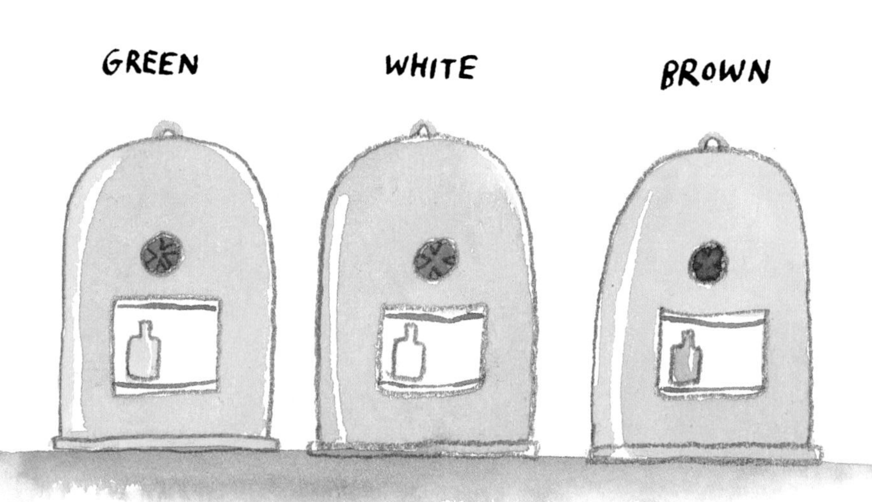

Collection points for bottles are sometimes called 'bottle banks'.

What if, after your bottle got washed it continued along the conveyor with thousands of other bottles...to be smashed into smithereens?

magnet
glass crusher

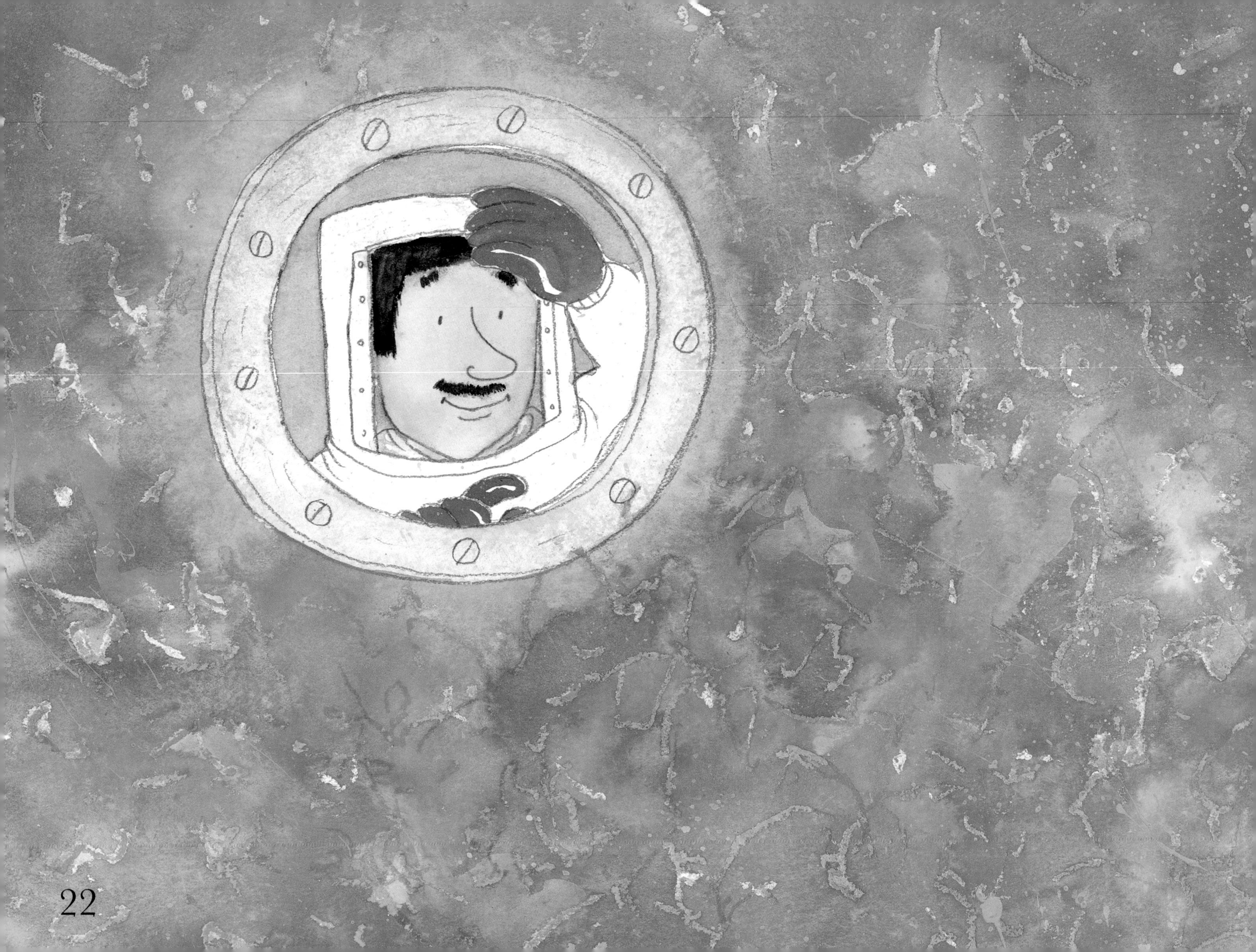

What if, the crushed bottles were sent to a furnace to be melted down into a red hot soup of liquid glass.

Recycled glass can be used for making new bottles, paint for road markings and fibre glass.

Fibre glass is used for making cars, planes and many other things.

Wait a minute!
What if, just before your bottle was crushed and melted down someone spotted your message?

some glass bottles, mostly green ones contain quite a lot of recycled glass already.

ello!
If you find this
bottle – let
me know!
address is:

What if, some day you got a parcel in the post from a far-away country? And when you opened it you found a shiny, new, green bottle with your boat, and a message inside!

Hi Kid!
Recycle your own rubbish next time!

Love
from Joe
(and everyone at the bottle factory)

Many everyday things can be recycled instead of thrown away. Perhaps there are some collection sites near you?

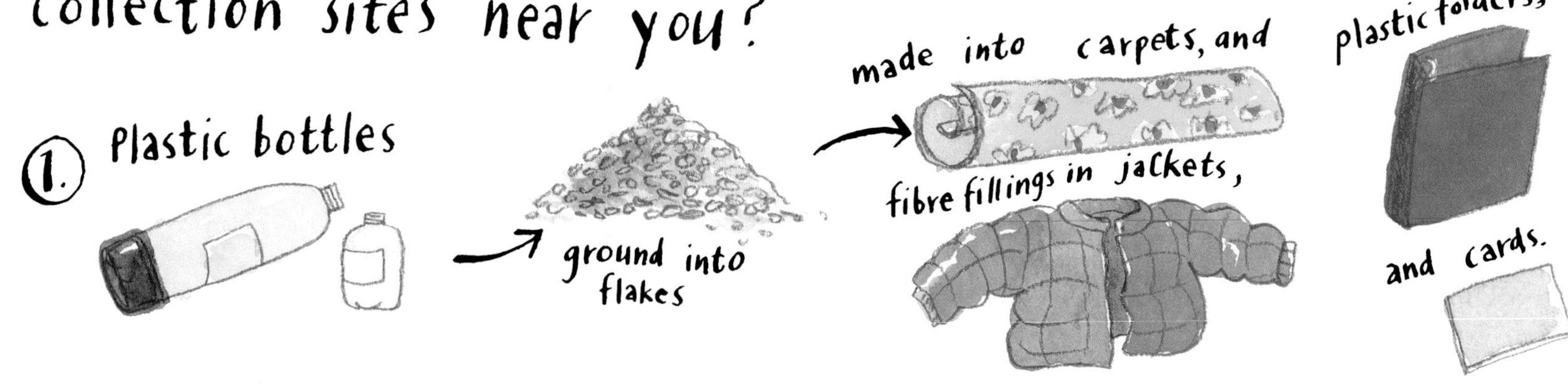

4. Glass
crushed into powder
melted and made into new bottles
or
made into paint for road markings
and road signs
or
made into fibreglass
5. Tyres
melted down
made into rubber mats
and running tracks.
6. Newspapers
baled up
pulped into liquid paper at papermill
made into phonebooks and new newspapers.

Helpful words

Cullet is the proper name for crushed glass before it gets melted.

Energy is the power to make things work. We need energy for light and heat, to work machines in factories, and to run vehicles like cars, trucks and planes. A lot of energy is used making glass bottles!

Furnace is like a very, very hot oven which melts down glass or metal into liquid.

Pollution is the poison and mess in the air, land and sea created by our rubbish. Pollution can kill plants and animals, it can harm us too.

Re-use is when something is used again instead of being thrown away – like mixing paint in an old jam jar or re-using an envelope to save paper.

Recycle is when you make something new from unwanted, empty or thrown-away things. For example, empty bottles can be melted down and made into new ones.

Resources are the Earth's raw materials such as wood, coal, rock and oil that we use to make everyday things. We must use Earth's resources carefully. What would we do without them?